Such Devoted Sisters

A Sister's Treasury

A sister can be seen as someone
who is both ourselves
and very much not ourselves—
a special kind of double.

—Toni Morrison

Such Devoted Sisters

A Sister's Treasury

by Mary Engelbreit
with Patrick Regan

**Andrews McMeel
Publishing**

Kansas City

05 06 07 08 09 EPB 10 9 8 7 6 5 4 3 2 1

Library of Congress Control Number: 2005924769

Compiled by Patrick Regan
Edited by Polly Blair

ISBN-13: 978-0-7407-5011-3
ISBN-10: 0-7407-5011-9

www.andrewsmcmeel.com

There were never such devoted Sisters.

for my mother, Mary Lois, and her sister, Audrey Ann

Table of Contents

Introduction

I am the eldest of three sisters (which sounds only slightly better than saying "oldest of three sisters"), and only two years separate me from the next oldest, Alexa. My youngest sister, Peggy, was born ten years after me.

When we were growing up, our house was on the edge of a wooded area and we'd spend countless hours playing in the woods, the creek, and later the construction sites that surrounded our suburban home. I freely admit that—whether because I was the oldest or because I was the bossiest—I was usually the leader of the small band of kids that roamed the woods and backyards of our neighborhood. But Alexa was always right by my side.

As we grew older, our interests often took us in different directions. I still loved to chase around with Alexa and the other kids, but I also spent a lot of time alone. When I learned to read, I discovered an amazing new world and a new dimension of myself. I would get lost in books—often drawing pictures inspired by what I read. It's funny—I realize now that some of my favorite books as a little girl were about,

you guessed it, sisters. *Little Women, Little House on the Prairie*, Jane Austen's books . . . even during those hours when I wasn't spending time with my "real" sisters, I was still surrounding myself with sisters.

Today, my sisters and I all live within ten miles of each other, and rarely does a week go by that I don't see one or both of them.

Pulling this book together has given me a wonderful opportunity to think about the real meaning of sisters and the powerful nature of sisterhood. I was fortunate enough to have two sisters by blood, but I am also tremendously lucky to count among my friends some amazing women that I have known since we were all little girls. They too are my sisters. And this book is a loving tribute to all of them—my sisters by birth and by choice.

Yours,

Mary

or there is no friend like a sister
   In calm or stormy weather;
To cheer one on the tedious way,
   To fetch one if one goes astray,
To lift one if one totters down,
   To strengthen whilst one stands.

—Christina Rossetti

11

We are sisters.
We will always be sisters.
Our differences may never go away,
but neither, for me,
will our song.

—Elizabeth Fishel

Never praise a sister to a sister
in the hope of your compliments
reaching the proper ears.

—Rudyard Kipling

There is no outsider anywhere
who wouldn't appreciate and even envy
the tremendous advantage that sisters have,
if properly utilized, against all odds.

—Susan Ripps

13

School Days

Ah, school days—the ugly uniforms, the bizarre haircuts my mother would come up with the day before school picture day. While everyone is honor-bound to complain about their uniforms (and my mother had plenty to complain about, judging by the gym uniforms in this old photo of her and her classmates in the center), they are really a wonderful invention. Your brain is free from the tyranny of "What should I wear?" and "Do I look all right?", and you're good to go. You could always tell who had an older sister by the state of their uniform. You ripped out seams, you spilled things on it, you lost the patch—until it seemed that you had nothing left to hand down to your sister, but your mother does anyway.

Clark Expedition left
They travelled
miles in nearly 2½ years
Missouri River.
Indian.

ULE

9:05 a.m.   English
9:50 a.m.   P.E.
10:15 a.m.   Relig
11:15 a.m.   Ar
12:00 p.m.   L
12:50 p.m.
1:15 p.m.   Band
2:15 p.m.   Speech

artifacts
✕
days
Ocean.
Good!

Jefferson asked Lewis to head the

...Then came my sisters,

created by fairies who lived in Manhattan and retrieved by my parents, who always went over to the city to bring back the next one from the hospital, the factory where I imagined my sisters were made . . . .

As each new sister arrived, the bond among us grew stronger, especially after our mother left. We became like a hand, fingers moving and behaving on their own, yet functioning together. By the time Michele was born, the fifth and last cellular creation of our parents during their doomed thirteen-year marriage, the hand was complete, a final balance was achieved. Each one of us was essentially placed, becoming the sister the rest of us had been waiting to welcome into this world.

—Carol A. Ortlip, *We Became Like a Hand*

If the family were fruit, it would be an orange,
    a circle of sections, held together but separable—
  each segment distinct.
                                        —Letty Cottin Pogrebin

17

ecause You're My Sister

by Jan Miller Girando

The older we get, the wiser we are—
the more we value those few
who have always been there
to support and to care,
and to help with whatever we do.

Of course, there are pals
who have stood by our side,
and companions on whom we depend,
but those with a sister
have richly been blessed
with a lifelong advisor and friend.

Who else but a sister would share in the memories
made through our "growing up" years,
the pranks that we played,
the plans that we laid,
our homes and our dreams and our fears?

Who else but a sister would know how it feels
when life takes us over the brink?
And who else but a sister would listen with patience
and actually care what we think?

Who else cheers us on
when we're trying our best,
and the perks haven't yet come our way,
and offers encouraging words of support,
brightening even the cloudiest day?

Who else but a sister would rush to our side
when misfortune took us by surprise—
helping out, pitching in, through the thick, through the thin,
doing more than we might realize?

And who but a sister would share in our triumphs
with energy, interest, and zest,
enjoying our victories as if they were hers,
and pretending to be so impressed?

Relaxing is fun when a sister's around—
lots of good-natured kidding takes place!
We can be who we are, we can do what we want
or just give one another some space!

When we're trying to weasel our way out of scrapes
she just shrugs with a sisterly sigh . . .
and gets set to extend the warm hand of a friend
should our mischievous plans go awry!

We can fool other people, but never our sister—
she knows our ways inside and out.
We can go to great pains reinventing ourselves,
but she really knows what we're about!

That's why sisterly love is the rarest of gifts
and its worth is replenished anew
as in laughter and tears
we progress through the years—
I should know, 'cause my sister is you.

Sisterly Love

My sister Alexa and I shared everything—toys, clothes, a room, and eventually an apartment. We were different, but always so close! I depend on her a lot and really value her steadiness. There is nothing like having someone you grew up with who remembers the same things—parents, houses, pets, vacations, friends—to ground you in reality and keep things in perspective. Of course, her memories are all wrong and mine are dazzlingly correct in their detail, but still, it's comforting to know there is someone else in the world who can verify how wonderful our childhood was.

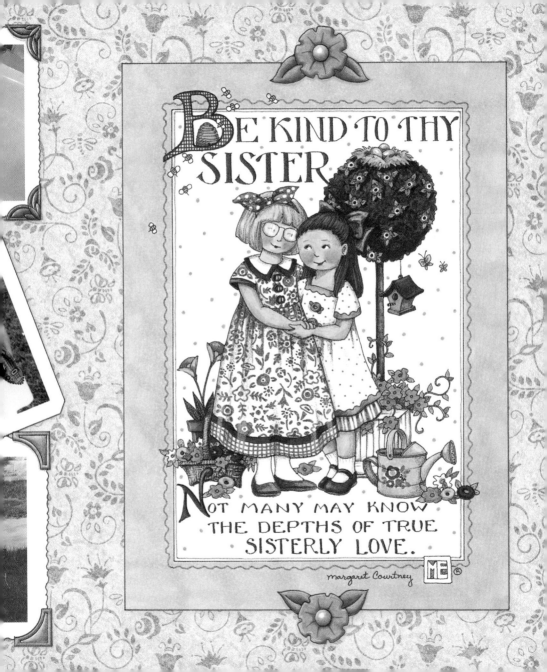

Sisters. Yes, we're just sisters.

Our story is not heroic, not even memorable.

But when I need support I sense you quietly by me.

I always will.

—Helen Thomson

She is your mirror,

shining back at you with a world of possibilities.
She is your witness, who sees you at your worst
and best, and loves you anyway.
She is your partner in crime, your midnight companion,
someone who knows when you are smiling,
even in the dark.
She is your teacher, your defense attorney,
your personal press agent, even your shrink.
Some days, she's the reason
you wish you were an only child.

—Barbara Alpert

Running Away

(excerpted from *About My Sisters*)
by Debra Ginsberg

Running away was probably my idea. I'd recently given Maya the kind of swell haircut that can only be fashioned by an eight-year-old and my mother was furious with me. I hated my new school. I hated that I was even in a new school. And I never liked the apartment; it was dark and claustrophobic. But even though I might have made the suggestion to run away, Maya had to have been amenable to it. I would never have gone anywhere without her.

It was wintertime and very cold outside, so we put on our fake camel-hair coats with impossible-to-fasten toggle buttons and our giant furry hats that tied with pom-poms. We packed a few items in our matching plastic purses and we were ready to go.

"We're running away," Maya told our father, who was in the living room watching *Star Trek*. He looked at our serious expressions and winter gear.

"Okay," he said. "Why are you going?"

"We don't like it here," I said.

"What about you, Maya?" he asked her.

"What Debra said," Maya answered.

I hoped he wouldn't try to convince her to stay, because Maya always folded long before I did and I wouldn't be able to leave without her. "Are you sure?" he asked both of us and we nodded solemnly.

"Okay," he said. "You'll probably need some money."

26

He dug into his pocket and gave us two quarters each. I was surprised, but also a little suspicious. I had expected resistance, some kind of protestation, or at least a plea to reconsider. I thought he was making it all a bit too easy.

Nevertheless, my mind went to the vending machines in the lobby. There were potato chips and chocolate milk. Fifty cents would come in handy. Maya and I tucked the money into our purses and stood by the front door.

"Okay, bye-bye," our father said, and turned back to his show. I noticed that Maya had started watching as well and was becoming distracted from our mission. She's always been a big *Star Trek* fan.

"Let's go," I told her.

Once we were outside in the hallway, we hesitated for a moment, anticipating that our father would stop pretending he didn't care and come out after us as soon as we closed the door, but no. There was nothing coming through that door except the tinny TV sound of a transporter beaming someone up from a hostile planet. And so we were off, marching down the hall to the elevator. That was where we ran into real trouble.

Neither Maya nor I could reach the elevator call button. Both of us tried reaching, stretching, and jumping, all to no avail. It never occurred to either one of us to look for the stairwell. We'd never used or seen stairs in this building. We lived on the tenth floor and assumed the elevator to be the only means of escape.

"What are we going to do now?" Maya asked me.

"Let's go ask for help," I said.

Back we went to the apartment.

"Did you change your mind?" our father asked.

"We can't reach the elevator," Maya said. "Can you come and help us?"

Our father had already been so willing and helpful, I was sure that he'd call the elevator for us at the next commercial, so what he said next came as a shock.

"No," he said. "If you want to run away, you're going to have to do it yourselves. And if you can't even reach the elevator, maybe you're not big enough to be running away."

We went back outside, back to the elevator, and still could find no way to get to the button. Sweating in our coats and hats, we were forced to admit we were beaten and go back to the apartment with our pom-poms between our legs. I was miserable, stewing in humiliation. I threw myself on my bed, coat still on, as if some miracle might happen and I'd be spirited away. Maya was no more than five years old at the time and her interest in running away had already waned, but she hated to see me upset or unable to handle any situation. It rattled her and she couldn't get comfortable until she knew I was all right.

Sisters

by Irving Berlin

Sisters, sisters,
There were never such devoted sisters,
Never had to have a chaperone, No sir,
I'm there to keep my eye on her.
Caring, sharing,
Every little thing that we are wearing—
When a certain gentleman arrived from Rome,
She wore the dress, and I stayed home.
All kinds of weather, we stick together,
The same in the rain and sun—
Two different faces, but in tight places
We think and we act as one.
Those who've seen us
Know that not a thing could come between us—
Many men have tried to split us up, but no one can.
Lord help the mister who comes between me and my sister
And Lord help the sister, who comes between me and my man.

Babes in Toyland

We had lots of family traditions at Christmastime. When Alexa and I were really little and living in our first house, the neighborhood would invite Santa with his horse-drawn carriage to come visit and give rides around the lane and pass out candy. When we got older, we would go downtown to the big department stores, visit whatever amazing Santaland they had cooked up that year, and then go out for dinner at my father's elegant club. On the way home, we would drive past all the houses with their Christmas light displays and choose our favorites. When I was ten, my sister Peggy was born, and just as Alexa and I were *almost* too cool to believe anymore, we got to start all over again with our baby sister!

JUST FOR YOU,

My sister taught me everything I need to know,
and she was only in the sixth grade at the time.

—Linda Sunshine

A sister smiles when one tells one's stories
for she knows where the decoration has been added.

—Chris Montaigne

If you don't understand how a woman
could both love her sister dearly
and want to wring her neck at the same time,
then you were probably an only child.

—Linda Sunshine

My Sister and Me

by Kate Holly

When we were very young . . .
And lost in play
Of endless summer days,
I never stopped to think about
how much it meant to me
to have you as my sister.

After all, there was so much to do . . .
Tea parties to attend,
Trees to climb,
Bubbles to blow,
Fireflies to chase,
And secrets to share.

And through it all—adventures big and small—
We were always side-by-side.

There were never two like me and you . . .
Whispering low under the covers long after bedtime,
Giggling at private jokes no one else would understand . . .
We had a language all our own.
Like any strong-willed young women,
We had our occasional differences of opinion.
But by the end of the day,
    we'd always find common ground . . .
And come back around again to each other.

Big sisters are the crabgrass
in the lawn of life.

—Charles M. Schulz

The Sisters You Choose

I have a great group of friends from childhood that I still see. Two of them, Chris Handlan and Maria Brennan, I have known since babyhood because our mothers were friends. We all lived in the same neighborhood, walked to and from school together, went to Brownies together (my mother was the Brownie leader one year, and to my mortification, would have us memorize poems every meeting— that's the troop in our backyard), and did all the things sisters-in-spirit do. Others, like Laurie Baker in the top photo, I met in grade school. Different uniforms, same kind of friendships. Just like real sisters we speak in shorthand, because we all know everything worth knowing about each other.

The Girls

Only a sister can compare
the sleek body that now
exists with the chubby body
hidden underneath.
Only a sister knows about former pimples,
failing math, and underwear
kicked under the bed.

—Laura Tracy

To Anna

by Louisa May Alcott

Sister, dear, when you are lonely,
Longing for your distant home,
And the images of loved ones
Warmly to your heart shall come,
Then, mid tender thoughts and fancies,
Let one fond voice say to thee,
"Ever when your heart is heavy,
Anna, dear, then think of me."

Think how we two have together
Journeyed onward day by day,
Joys and sorrows ever sharing,
While the swift years roll away.
Then may all the sunny hours
Of our youth rise up to thee,
And when your heart is light and happy,
Anna, dear, then think of me.

Me and My Shadow

by Sheila Dolan

excerpt from *Satellite Sisters' UnCommon Senses*

Everybody needs a best friend. Most of the time, I had one, but when they weren't around, I had Monica. We were a year apart in age and we went through all the trials and tribulations that best friends endure and then some. A best friend goes home to her own house at the end of the school day, but your buddy sister stays with you for the full twenty-four hours. I'm sure there were some nights Monica went to bed wishing we weren't related but, in the light of day, when she needed a certain pair of jeans that I owned, our special relationship was instantly restored.

Monica and I gravitated toward each other, I think, because we were both interested in things, while our big sisters Julie and Liz were concerned with ideas and principles. The only belief the two of us held was that everybody deserved a decent outfit, so on a daily basis you have to grab for whatever clothes you think you need. Not everyone in the family shared this belief, so the two of us often ran into a little trouble fulfilling our credo. I admired Monica's courage in the face of danger, because Lord knows I put her in some tight spots when we were teens.

Monica was the perfect ally and partner in crime. She kept quiet while I tried to explain my way out of situations, and she understood my pain when I didn't succeed. She came to my aid when I found myself completely defeated after a botched clothes heist. Sometimes, I would make it as far as Julie's closet when Mom would walk in with some fresh laundry and bust me. I taught Monica all I knew about layering (wearing borrowed clothing items under your own), early morning raids, and footwear.

Monica and I shared the proletariat's view: Life was simply harder for the two of us. We needed to rebel against the forces that controlled us, but mainly, we just needed our stuff. I didn't feel any big-sister superiority over Monica. Maybe that was because I was always getting in trouble and, as a result, I knew I could always count on Monica for getting in trouble with me, because of me, or instead of me. It could have been routine grumbling about doing a chore or babysitting Brendan, but if the two of us were involved, the incident inevitably escalated. We just couldn't let things be. Julie's savoir faire didn't rub off

on us, nor did we exhibit any of Liz's good sense. We were a dangerous combination of clumsiness and bad judgment.

It was always "Sheila's in trouble" or "Monica and Sheila are in trouble" or "Monica's in trouble; where's Sheila?" The best part of getting in trouble was having someone there to commiserate with after the fact. It was at those times when my affection for Monica grew even deeper. She was probably thinking, "Better you than me," as she sat at the end of my bed, flipping through *Seventeen* and looking up every few minutes as I railed against humanity, but Monica made me feel like a victor even though I had just been grounded.

"Club"

Once a month for the past (almost) sixty years, my mother went to her "Club." "Club" is sisterhood at its finest—a group of girls who met in grade school and went on to support each other their entire lives. They would get together for dinner and drinks, alternating houses each month. Sometimes they would vacation together. They always loved each other and helped each other through weddings, births, children, grandchildren, and deaths. What a wonderful way my sisters and I learned about friendships! No wonder my friends and sisters are the center of my life today.

TALLY

TABLE N°   COUPLE N°

We are givers
and receivers
of female wisdom
and are constantly
learning from
each other.

—Debra Ginsberg

For Better or Worse

Even the bride with the best intentions, especially back when my friends and I were bridesmaids, manages to pick out a dress you would never wear again in a million years. Actually, my sisters (in the photo below), were able to wear theirs again when they were pregnant! My friend Chris was married at a country church and the dresses fit right in, although I begged her to forget the bonnets. Oh well. It's a universal badge of courage for sisters and friends—the best thing to do is just have a good attitude about it and know you're wearing it for someone you love.

ONE LOSES MANY LAUGHS BY NOT LAUGHING AT ONESELF.
SARA JEANNETTE DUNCAN

For Sale

by Shel Silverstein

One sister for sale!
One sister for sale!
One crying and spying young sister for sale!
I'm really not kidding,
So who will start the bidding?
Do I hear a dollar?
A nickle?
A penny?
Oh, isn't there, isn't there,
isn't there any
One kid who will buy this old
sister for sale,
This crying and spying young
sister for sale?

Sisters is probably
the most competitive relationship
within the family,
but once sisters are grown,
it becomes the strongest relationship.

—Margaret Mead

There are all those early memories;

one cannot get another set;

one has only those.

—Willa Cather

The only one I could wholly, totally confide in,

lives in the same house with me,

and not only never has, but never will,

leave me one secret to tell her.

—Frances Burney D'Arblay

You can kid the world
but not your sister.

—Charlotte Gray

If sisters were free to express
how they really feel,
parents would hear this:
"Give me all the attention
and all the toys
and send Rebecca
to live with Grandma."

—Linda Sunshine

Help one another,
is part of the religion
of sisterhood.

—Louisa May Alcott

Acknowledgments

Andrews McMeel Publishing has made every effort
to contact the copyright holders.

Page 16 from *We Became Like a Hand* by Carol A. Ortlip
Copyright © 2002 by Carol A. Ortlip
Published by The Ballantine Publishing Group

Page 26 from *About My Sisters* by Debra Ginsberg
Copyright © 2004 Debra Ginsberg
Reprinted by permission of HarperCollins Publishers

Page 46 from *Uncommon Senses* by the Satellite Sisters, LLC.
Copyright © 2001 by Satellite Sisters, LLC
Published by Riverhead Books, a member of Penguin Putnam, Inc.

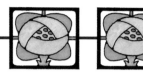

Illustrations

The original Ann Estelle (center),
with her sister Grace, and sister-in-law Josephine